FROM THE MIXED-UP FILES OF MRS. BASIL E. FRANKWEILER

by
E. L. Konigsburg

D1799654

Student Packet

Written by
Jean Jamieson

Contains masters for:

3	Prereading Activities
7	Writing Activities
4	Math Activities
1	Illustration and Writing Activity
2	Comprehension Activities
3	Writing Poetry Activities
4	Vocabulary Activities
3	Art / Illustration Activities
1	Thinking Activity
1	Teacher Suggestions for Assessment
2	Comprehension Quizzes
	Detailed Answer Key

PLUS

Teacher Note
Selected activities, quizzes, and test questions in this Novel Units® Student Packet are labeled with the appropriate reading/language arts skills for quick reference. These skills can be found above quiz/test questions or sections and in the activity headings.

Note
The text used to prepare this guide was the Dell Yearling softcover, © 1967 by E. L. Konigsburg. The page references may differ in the hardcover or other paperback editions.

Please note: Please assess the appropriateness of this book for the age level and maturity of your students prior to reading and discussing it with your class.

To order, contact your local school supply store, or—

Novel Units, Inc.
P.O. Box 97
Bulverde, TX 78163-0097

Web site: novelunits.com

Note to the Teacher

Selected activities, quizzes, and test questions in this Novel Units® Student Packet are labeled with the following reading/language arts skills for quick reference. These skills can be found above quiz/test questions or sections and in the activity headings.

Basic Understanding: The student will demonstrate a basic understanding of written texts. The student will:
- use a text's structure or other sources to locate and recall information (Locate Information)
- determine main idea and identify relevant facts and details (Main Idea and Details)
- use prior knowledge and experience to comprehend and bring meaning to a text (Prior Knowledge)
- summarize major ideas in a text (Summarize Major Ideas)

Literary Elements: The student will apply knowledge of literary elements to understand written texts. The student will:
- analyze characters from a story (Character Analysis)
- analyze conflict and problem resolution (Conflict/Resolution)
- recognize and interpret literary devices (flashback, foreshadowing, symbolism, simile, metaphor, etc.) (Literary Devices)
- consider characters' points of view (Point of View)
- recognize and analyze a story's setting (Setting)
- understand and explain themes in a text (Theme)

Analyze Written Texts: The student will use a variety of strategies to analyze written texts. The student will:
- identify the author's purpose (Author's Purpose)
- identify cause and effect relationships in a text (Cause/Effect)
- identify characteristics representative of a given genre (Genre)
- interpret information given in a text (Interpret Text)
- make and verify predictions with information from a text (Predictions)
- sequence events in chronological order (Sequencing)
- identify and use multiple text formats (Text Format)
- follow written directions and write directions for others to follow (Follow/Write Directions)

Critical Thinking: The student will apply critical-thinking skills to analyze written texts. The student will:
- write and complete analogies (Analogies)
- find similarities and differences throughout a text (Compare/Contrast)
- draw conclusions from information given (Drawing Conclusions)
- make and explain inferences (Inferences)
- respond to texts by making connections and observations (Making Connections)
- recognize and identify the mood of a text (Mood)
- recognize an author's style and how it affects a text (Style)
- support responses by referring to relevant aspects of a text (Support Responses)
- recognize and identify the author's tone (Tone)
- write to entertain, such as through humorous poetry or short stories (Write to Entertain)
- write to express ideas (Write to Express)
- write to inform (Write to Inform)
- write to persuade (Write to Persuade)
- demonstrate understanding by creating visual images based on text descriptions (Visualizing)
- practice math skills as they relate to a text (Math Skills)

Name_____

Proverbs

*Be a friend to yourself
and others will befriend you.*
Scottish

A proverb is a short, popular saying that expresses some obvious truth. The following proverbs are about <u>friends</u>. Read the proverbs. Choose the one that you like best. Tell what the proverb means to you. Make an illustration to go with your explanation.

1. *A friend in need is a friend indeed.*
English
2. *A friend is better than a thousand silver pieces.*
Greek
3. *A friend is not so easy to find as to lose.*
Jamaican
4. *A friend is to be taken with his faults.*
Portuguese
5. *A friend you get for nothing; an enemy has to be bought.*
Yiddish
6. *A good friend is better than silver and gold.*
Dutch
7. *A good friend never offends.*
English

The proverb I like best is # _____. In my own words, it means: _____

_____

Write an original proverb: _____

_____

A FRIEND IS A PERSON WITH WHOM YOU DARE TO BE YOURSELF.

From the Mixed-Up Files of Mrs. Basil E. Frankweiler
Student Worksheet #2
Prereading
(Prior Knowledge/Visualizing)

Picture This

Create a visual that illustrates "good friend" qualities. You may want to use humor in a cartoon or comic strip, a poster, an ad, a bulletin or notice, or some other method that suits the way you wish to express your thoughts. Use as few words as possible, relying more on the visual to express your opinion.

A FRIEND IS ONE WHO COMES TO YOU WHEN ALL OTHERS LEAVE.

4

Name_____

Friendship

Well-known authors have given opinions regarding friendship in their writings.

Read the following excerpts from the prose and poetry of the authors noted. Choose one. Give your opinion of the statement, and explain your feelings regarding what the statement says about friendship. Then make your own statement about friendship.

Shakespeare: *Most friendship is feigning...*(As You Like It)

Francis Bacon: *There is little friendship in the world, and least of all between equals.*
(Of Followers and Friends)

Orson Welles: *When you are down and out something always turns up—and it's usually the noses of your friends.* (Interview)

La Rouchefoucauld: *What men call friendship is only a reciprocal conciliation of interests, an exchange of good offices; it is in short simply a form of barter from which self-love always expects to gain something.* (Maxims)

Ovid: *The vulgar herd estimate friendship by its advantages.* (Epistolae ex Ponto II)

Samuel Johnson: *Friendship is seldom lasting but between equals.* (The Rambler, No. 64)

My Statement:

FRIENDSHIP IS INCLUDING OTHER PEOPLE'S HAPPINESS IN YOUR OWN.

Name_____

That Reminds Me Of...

To yourself or to a classmate, quietly read aloud the letter that Mrs. Basil E. Frankweiler writes to her lawyer. Do this with expression. <u>Notice</u> <u>how</u> <u>you</u> <u>feel</u> <u>as</u> <u>you</u> <u>are</u> <u>reading</u> <u>the</u> <u>letter.</u>

People are often compared to animals, plants, and other things. For example:

"He was a bear this morning."   "She sings like a bird."
"She runs as fast as a deer."   "He is as happy as a lark."
"He is growing like a weed."   "She looks as fresh as a daisy."

Remembering the feeling that the letter evokes, what would you choose to represent Mrs. Frankweiler? Make an illustration that shows your choice.

THE SECRET OF FRIENDSHIP IS COURTESY.

From the Mixed-Up Files of Mrs. Basil E. Frankweiler

It Costs HOW Much?

This book has a copyright date of 1967. In Chapter 1, the prices for several items are given. Do some research to determine the current cost (in your locale) of each item listed. (You may substitute a local transportation carrier [i.e., a bus] for the train, and a large city near you for New York City.) Record your findings on the chart below.

Continue to use the chart as you read the story. Interview adults you know. Do they remember the cost of other items at approximately the same time in history? Record any additional information that you are able to gather. Share this information with others.

Name of Item	1967 cost	current cost	amt. of increase or decrease	% change
Train fare to NY	one way/full fare $1.60			
Hot Fudge Sundae Hot Fudge (Sale)	$.40 $.27			
Allowance	$.50 per week (Claudia, age 12) $.25 per week (Jamie, age 9)			

Allowance?

It is 1967. Claudia receives fifty cents weekly as her allowance (page 8). Interview some adults you know. Make an allowance survey. For example, ask:

Did you receive an allowance? yes_____ no_____   If yes, what was the amount per week? _____ How old were you then? _____

Enter your results on the graph below.

$ 3.00						
$ 2.75						
$ 2.50						
$ 2.25						
$ 2.00						
$ 1.75						
$ 1.50						
$ 1.25						
$ 1.00						
$ .75						
$ .50						
$ .25						
$ .00						
Age:	7 years	8 years	9 years	10 years	11 years	12 years

Make summary statements about the information presented on the graph. (Use the back of your paper.)

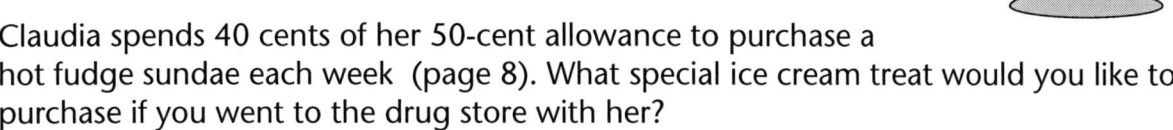

Gooey! Gooey!

Claudia spends 40 cents of her 50-cent allowance to purchase a
hot fudge sundae each week (page 8). What special ice cream treat would you like to
purchase if you went to the drug store with her?

Just in case the people in charge of the soda fountain don't know how to make your favorite
treat, have the instructions handy. Write them out in the space below. Make illustrations to go
with them.

*How to Make*_____

Fun Food Freezer

In order to save money for the adventure, Claudia eats Good Humor ice cream bars from the family freezer rather than purchasing her usual hot fudge sundae each week (page 8).

If the choices were up to you, what additional kinds of fun food would you put in the freezer?

_____

_____

_____

The words Fun Food Freezer, when said quickly, become a tongue twister. Try to say the words as fast as you can three times, without making a mistake. After you can do that, increase the length of the tongue twister by adding another word that begins with the letter/sound **F**. Keep adding words. How many words are you able to include in your tongue twister? How fast can you say it?
For example:

Fun Food Freezer
Freaky Fun Food Freezer
Fast Freaky Fun Food Freezer
Forever Fast Freaky Fun Food Freezer

Below, create a cartoon, riddle, or joke about the Forever Fast Freaky Fun Food Freezer.

Metropolitan Museum of Art
New York City

The Metropolitan Museum of Art in New York City is the largest art museum in the United States. It includes more than 2 million works of art. The City of New York owns the building. The collections belong to a corporation that runs the museum under a charter granted in 1870. For more than a century the City of New York and the trustees of The Metropolitan Museum of Art have been partners in bringing the Museum's services to the public.

The complex of buildings in Central Park is the property of the City, and the City provides funds for the museum's heat, light, and power. The City also pays for about half the costs of maintenance and security for the facility and its collections.

The collections themselves are held in trust by the trustees. The trustees, in turn, are responsible for meeting all expenses connected with conservation, education, special exhibitions, acquisitions, scholarly publications, and related professional and administrative activities including security and maintenance costs not covered by the City.

The museum offers concerts and lectures in a seven-hundred-seat auditorium. The collections include Egyptian Art, Asian Art, Musical Instruments, Arms and Armor, European Paintings, Decorative Arts, Medieval Art, Ancient Near Eastern Art, Greek and Roman Art, Islamic Art, and Twentieth Century Art.

In sum, the Metropolitan represents a rare combination of public and private resources united in the effort to enrich the lives of all who visit the museum.

Answer TRUE (T) or FALSE (F) to the following questions:

1. The Metropolitan Museum is an art museum._____

2. The City of New York owns the museum._____

3. The complex of buildings is in Central Park._____

4. The City of New York is responsible for all of the expenses of the Museum. _____

5. The Museum houses a collection of musical instruments._____

Which exhibit would you visit first? Why?

The First Day

Claudia and Jamie end the first day of "the greatest adventure" in their lives in a bed in the Metropolitan Museum of Art in New York City (page 42). They have shared experiences and feelings, and have become a real team during this busy day.

Use the **quatrain** form of poetry to sum up their first day. (The quatrain is a poem written in four lines, and may be rhymed or unrhymed. When rhymed, there can be a variety of rhyming patterns, such as *aabb, abab, abcb, aaaa,* etc.)

Examples of quatrain poetry:		YOUR QUATRAIN POETRY

In Bed

Sleeping in an old, old bed;	a
Dreaming of the days ahead.	a
Claudia! Jamie! Do you care	b
That no one knows you're there?	b

Central Park

Tired children, with great plans,	a
Sleeping. Sleeping in the dark	b
Of the Museum of Art. Silence,	c
Even in the heart of Central Park.	b

Name_____

Meanwhile...

What do you think might be happening at the Kincaid residence as Claudia and Jamie end their day at the Museum?

Use words to create a picture as you describe a detailed scene at the Kincaid home. Use descriptive words to communicate the feelings of those involved. Appeal to the senses and emotions of those who will read your work.

_____

_____

_____

_____

_____

_____

_____

_____

_____

_____

_____

_____

_____

_____

_____

_____

_____

_____

_____

_____

Name_____

Michelangelo
Word Search Puzzle

Do the word search. Write down the letters that have not been used, starting at the top and working left to right in each row. Group the letters into words and complete this sentence.

Michelangelo was _____.

```
M I C H E L A N G E L O S
R A N A T O M Y I A A T I
E R R S C U L P T O R O S
N T M B A T N O A G C M T
A I F O L D I R L R H B I
I S P O W E R O Y A I F N
S T D A V I D M N N T L E
S M A N I A Y E T D E O C
A P P R E N T I C E C R H
N A L P O E T I E U T E A
C J U L I U S N C R T N P
E M O V E M E N T A S C E
B U O N A R R O T I N E L
```

WORDS TO FIND

MICHELANGELO	ARTIST
SCULPTOR	PAINT
ARCHITECT	POET
ITALY	RENAISSANCE
ANATOMY	SISTINE CHAPEL
ROME	JULIUS
VATICAN	DAVID
TOMB	OLD
BUONARROTI	FLORENCE
APPRENTICE	MOVEMENT
POWER	GRANDEUR
MARBLE	ACTION

**Do some research.
Find out more about Michelangelo.**

Michelangelo
Crossword Puzzle

The words used are associated with Michelangelo: *apprentice, Buonarroti, Caprese, complicated, designed, fresco, grandeur, Julius, massive, Michelangelo, patron, prophecy, Renaissance, sculptor, Sibyl, style, tomb, Vatican.* Match each word with its clue and fit it into the puzzle.

Across

1. A great leader of the Italian Renaissance.
5. female prophet
6. one who learns from practical experience
8. Papal headquarters in Rome
11. particular manner/technique in which something is done
13. family (surname) name of Michelangelo
14. artist who produces works of sculpture
16. prediction of something to come
17. art of painting on freshly spread moist lime plaster

Down

1. impressively large
2. magnificence
3. created
4. transitional movement in Europe
7. supporter
9. village of Michelangelo's birth
10. Pope who first brought Michelangelo to Rome
12. consisting of parts intricately combined
15. place of interment

Name_____

"Angel"

"Jamie, let's do it now. Let's skip learning everything about everything in the museum. Let's concentrate on the statue." Claudia to Jamie, page 62

Be a sleuth along with Claudia and Jamie. Record the information and clues about the statue "Angel" as the story progresses.

page #	clue

Cinquain Poetry

Surrounded by beauty wherever they go in the museum, Claudia and Jamie enjoy attending the special lectures given for children.

Imagine that you are with Claudia and Jamie, as they go from one gallery to the next, and you gaze upon some paintings that really interest you. Choose a painting to describe, one that you remember or have seen somewhere. Use the cinquain poetry form.

Cinquain is an unrhymed form of poetry consisting of five prescribed ideas. The form consists of syllables arranged in a two, four, six, eight, two-syllable pattern. The first line announces the topic.

2–syllable word or words announcing topic
4 syllables describing topic
6 syllables expressing action
8 syllables expressing feeling
2 syllables/ending/ synonym for topic

Fruit bowl
Smooth velvety
Fragrance wafting from cores
Hunger gnawing on my backbone
Tasty

Create a cinquain of your own. Use a painting or a piece of art as your topic.

_____2

_____4

_____6

_____8

_____2

_____

Homesick

Claudia and Jamie think about home, and of how things are going quite well for them in the museum. Claudia tells Jamie,"Heaven knows, we're well trained. Just look how nicely we've managed. It's really their [parents] fault if we're not homesick." (pp. 85-87)

Have you ever been homesick? What thoughts and feelings does the word bring to mind?

An **acrostic** is a form of poetry that may be rhymed or unrhymed, and has the topic printed vertically, letter by letter. Each letter is used to construct a word, phrase or sentence which describes the topic, in this case, HOMESICK. Think of a word, phrase, or sentence that begins with the letter on each line. Each line should say something meaningful about HOMESICK.

H_____

O_____

M_____

E_____

S_____

I_____

C_____

K_____

Name_____

Use the seven pieces of the tangram square to make the lady. (There is a tangram square on page 20.)

The Medieval Lady Tangram

Tangram Square Activities

1. If the small square piece of the tangram square weighs one pound, what is the weight of each of the other six pieces? What is the total weight of the square?
    Small Triangles: _____   Medium Triangle: _____   Total: _____
    Parallelogram: _____   Large Triangles: _____

2. How much is the tangram square worth if the smallest triangle has a value of $1,000.00? _____What is the value of each piece of the tangram square?
    Small Triangles: _____   Medium Triangle: _____
    Parallelogram: _____   Large Triangles: _____   Square: _____

3. What is the value of each piece of the tangram square if the whole square is worth $16.00?
    Small Triangles: _____
    Medium Triangle: _____
    Parallelogram: _____
    Large Triangles: _____
    Square: _____

4. If the smallest triangle of the tangram square has a value of 2/5 , what is the value of each piece of the tangram square? What is the total value of the square?
    Small Triangles: _____
    Medium Triangle: _____
    Parallelogram: _____
    Large Triangles: _____
    Square: _____
    TOTAL: _____

Make Your Mark

Claudia and Jamie discover a clue about the angel statue, page 92. After doing some research, they decide that the statue has Michelangelo's stonemason's mark on the bottom.

Follow the directions given and make some art dough. Model this dough as you would any clay to make something that is pleasing to you. Put a special "mark" on the bottom, so that it may be identified as your creation. Air dry for a few days. Remember to turn the dough sculpture for even drying, so that all surfaces are exposed to the air at some time.

Basic Art Dough (non-edible)

Materials:
4 cups flour
1 cup iodized salt
1 3/4 cups warm water
bowl
newspaper
aluminum foil
pencil

Process:
1. Cover the work area with newspaper.
2. Place all materials on the newspaper.
3. Mix all ingredients in bowl.
4. Knead 10 minutes.
5. Model as with any clay.
6. Put "mark" on bottom of sculpture (use a pencil).
7. Place on a sheet of foil to dry.
8. Clean up the area.
9. Air dry for a few days.
10. Turn sculpture for even drying, exposing all surfaces to the air at some time.

Name_____

Misplaced Persons

Claudia and Jamie are very surprised to find Jamie's third-grade classmates visiting the Egyptian wing of the museum (pages 105–108).

Have you ever seen someone you know well in a special setting—such as a dentist, a doctor, a teacher—in a different setting? (example: seeing your dentist at the video arcade) How did you react? How did you feel? (We often get so used to seeing someone in a specific setting that we forget that this individual changes locations.)

Write about an imagined, humorous situation in which one or more persons are "misplaced."

_____

_____

_____

_____

_____

_____

_____

_____

_____

_____

_____

_____

_____

_____

_____

_____

_____

Name_____

Shapely Art

Imagine that before Claudia and Jamie leave for the day, they want to look at a painting that fascinates them. It is made entirely of shapes. They are going to try to count all of the different shapes.

Look at the print below. How many different shapes do you see? On another sheet of paper, make a list of the different shapes. Count each kind of shape, and record the number next to its name. Check with others. Did you get the same answer?

I'm Dreaming Of...

As Claudia and Jamie take the train to Farmington, Connecticut, Jamie thinks of having something special for lunch that day. Several choices come to his mind. One is pictured here. What is your opinion of this choice? Do you think this is a healthy choice? Why or why not?

_____

_____

_____

Make a healthy choice for yourself. Explain your reasons for making this choice, and for picking these particular foods. I would choose_____

_____

_____

Make a collage of healthy food choices. To make a collage, you will need heavyweight paper or cardboard, paste, scissors, scraps of all sorts, and pictures taken from magazines, newspapers, etc., of food items that you want to represent.

Arrange the pictures on the paper or cardboard, overlapping them. When you get an arrangement that you like, paste the pictures in place. Place items on the picture that will enhance it and go with the theme, or bring the items together into the theme (wrappers, cereal, popcorn, pretzels, pasta, string, yarn, etc.).

Name_____

Learn

Mrs. Frankweiler does not agree with Claudia, that something new should be learned each day. Mrs. Frankweiler tells Claudia, "…you should also have days when you allow what is already in you to swell up inside of you until it touches everything." Mrs. Frankweiler feels that, when the touching happens, what one has learned becomes an integral part of the person. Otherwise, one has just isolated facts that "rattle around" (page 153).

Do you agree with Claudia or Mrs. Frankweiler, or with neither of them? Explain your response. Give at least three good reasons to back up your point of view.

_____
_____
_____
_____
_____
_____
_____
_____
_____
_____
_____
_____
_____
_____
_____
_____
_____
_____
_____
_____

Name_____

From the Mixed-Up Files of Mrs. Basil E. Frankweiler
Student Worksheet #24
Chapter 9
(Making Connections)

Filing

Mrs. Frankweiler has an unusual filing system. However, she has a good reason for filing her things as she does.

How would you file the following articles? Make up and explain your own filing system for these articles.

"Stock a Pharmacy of Good Food"
"Put Stress to Work For You"
"Low Cholesterol Benefits Are Questioned"
"It's Not Just Baby Talk"
"I Wish I'd Had The Guts"
"Are We Still A Nation At Risk?"
"The Sound of Music: Inventor Provides a Pleasant Earful"
"Table Business in the Pocket"
"Desk For Success"
"Fast-Braking News"
"Green Architecture Comes of Age"
"Orcas in Captivity"
Time asks "Can Animals Talk?"
"Massive Suffering of Animals in Cross-Border Trade with Mexico"
"A Commonsense Approach to Pesticides"
"Yogurt: Bacteria to Basics"
"All Washed Up"
"Who Needs Help Interpreting the New Nutrition Labels & Why"
"The Heart of the Matter"
"Lifting Weight Myths"
"Monitor Troubles?"
"New Gear For Your Next Gig"
"Modem Manners"
"The Purpose of Toes"

Make a cartoon showing you doing some filing!

Name_____

Vocabulary Word Search Puzzle

Do the word search. Write down the letters that have not been used, starting at the top and working left to right in each row. Group the letters into words to find the hidden message.

Hidden Message: _____

```
C O N S C I E N C E C K C F
A O U T R A G E O U S A O A
L U M U T U A L L M A L U T
C O T M B O O D L E R E N I
U U G O O A U M S D C I T G
L S R I M T D A A I O D E U
A I T A C A I S R O P O R E
T A S O T E T O I C H S F I
E E S A N O S N N R A C E N
D T A E M E R G E E G O I S
T C O N S E N S U S U P T A
U E A B R A S I O N S E E N
M E T R O P O L I T A N D E
```

WORDS TO FIND

CONSCIENCE	CALCULATED
CURATORS	OUTRAGEOUS
SARCOPHAGUS	CONSENSUS
METROPOLITAN	KALEIDOSCOPE
COUNTERFEITED	COMMOTION
AUTOMAT	MUTUAL
ABRASIONS	BOODLE
MEDIOCRE	EMERGE
MASON	STONE
LOGIC	SARI
FATIGUE	INSANE

Some other things to do:
1. Put the words in reverse alphabetical order.
2. Define half the words.
3. Use half of the remaining words in sentences.

Vocabulary Crossword Puzzle

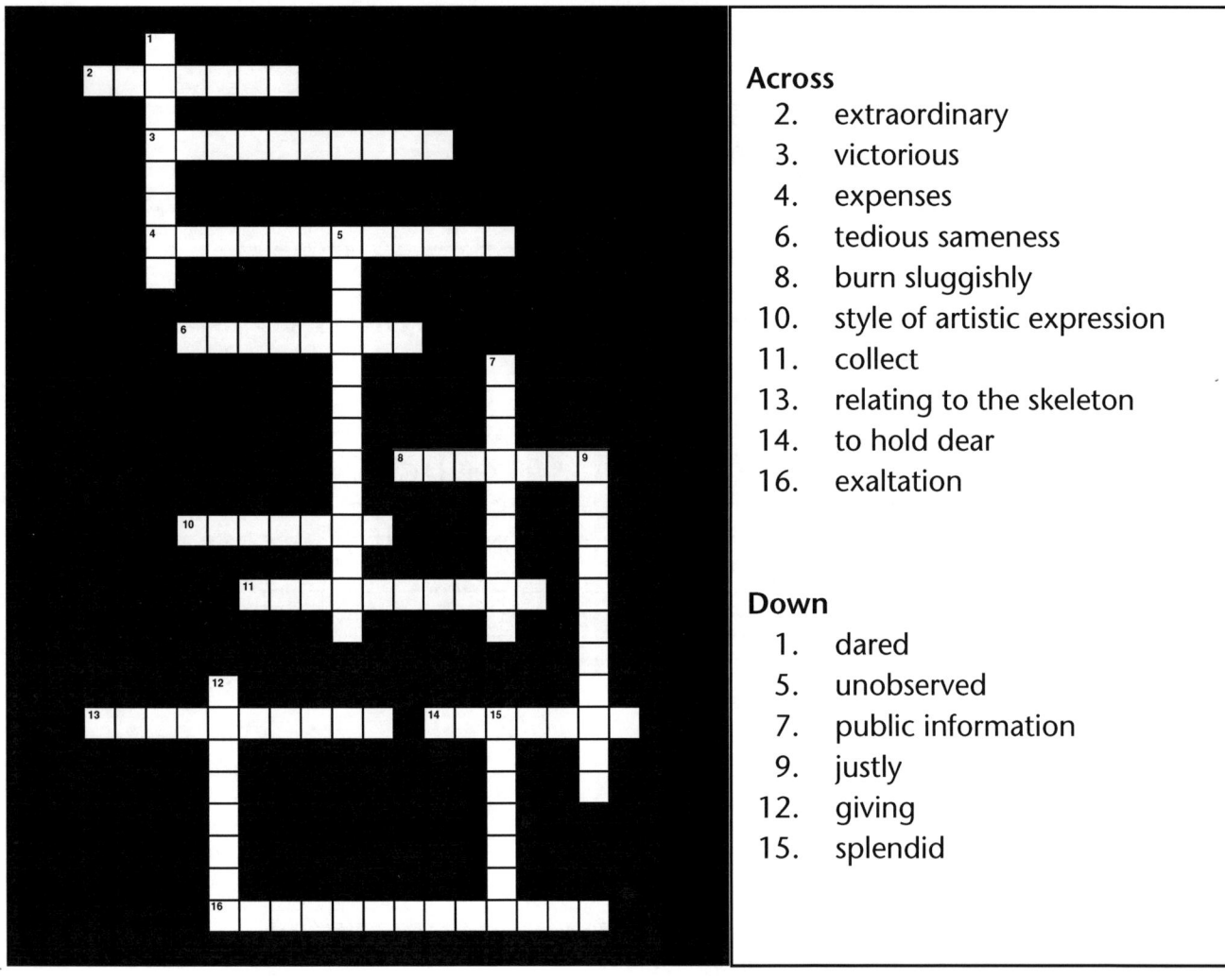

Across
2. extraordinary
3. victorious
4. expenses
6. tedious sameness
8. burn sluggishly
10. style of artistic expression
11. collect
13. relating to the skeleton
14. to hold dear
16. exaltation

Down
1. dared
5. unobserved
7. public information
9. justly
12. giving
15. splendid

Words Used
accumulate, awesome, baroque, cherish, donating, elegant, expenditures, glorification, inconspicuous, monotony, orthopedic, publicity, righteously, smolder, triumphant, ventured

Name_____

"The Greatest Adventure Of Our Lives"

Imagine that you are Claudia or Jamie, recording for Mrs. Frankweiler details of "the greatest adventure" of your life, and your feelings about it.

Write down what you will tell Mrs. Frankweiler so you won't forget the important impressions you had and the feelings you shared with your partner in this adventure. Also make a closing statement about what you have learned from this adventure. (Include what you learned about running away. Give the pros and cons.) Did the adventure change your life? If so, in what way?

_____

_____

_____

_____

_____

_____

_____

_____

_____

_____

_____

_____

_____

_____

_____

_____

Name_____

To The Student

This page is for you. You do not have to share it, turn it in, or even keep it. Please think about what Mrs. Frankweiler has to say:

About <u>secrets</u>: "I need having the secret more than I need the money." "Secrets are the kind of adventure she needs. Secrets are safe, and they do much to make you different. On the inside where it counts." (pages 148 & 150)

About <u>learning</u>: Mrs. Frankweiler feels that it is important to keep on learning, but that it is not necessary to learn something new each day—that there are times when each person needs to let the knowledge that has been accumulated "swell up inside" and become an integral part of the person. If that is not done, one has just a bunch of isolated facts that "rattle around" inside. (page 153)

About <u>cheating</u>: "Jamie, when the stakes are high, I never cheat. I consider myself too important to do that." (page 148)

About <u>happiness</u>: "Happiness is excitement that has found a settling down place, but there is always a little corner that keeps flapping around." (page 151)

<u>Claudia to Jamie as they search:</u> (page 144) "Five minutes of planning are worth fifteen minutes of just looking."

To The Teacher

The concluding activity may be used as the final test for the novel unit. The student uses the knowledge gained through reading the novel, interprets it, and makes use of that knowledge. Responsive feelings are explored and analyzed.

The following pages may be used as quiz pages if the teacher so desires:

a) Chapter 1, Worksheet #6, Allowance?—To make a survey and to use a bar graph to summarize the data.

b) Chapter 2, Worksheet #9, Metropolitan Museum of Art—To read for information.

c) Chapter 4, Worksheet #12, Michelangelo—To recognize words associated with Michelangelo; to group letters into words.

d) Chapter 4, Worksheet #13, Michelangelo—To match definition to word; to become familiar with words associated with Michelangelo.

e) Chapter 5, Worksheet #16, Homesick—To use an acrostic

f) Chapter 9, Worksheet #23, Learn—To explain and defend a point of view

g) Chapter 10, Worksheet #25, Vocabulary Word Search Puzzle—Vocabulary word recognition, grouping of letters into words, and word usage

h) Chapter 10, Worksheet #26, Vocabulary Crossword Puzzle—To match vocabulary words with definitions

Comprehension quizzes follow.

Name_____

(Main Idea and Details)
Directions: Read the information and fill in each blank space with a word, words or phrase that will make the information given complete and true to the story.

Sample: The name of this novel is <u>*From the Mixed-Up Files of Mrs. Basil E. Frankweiler*</u>.

1. Claudia Kincaid and younger brother, Jamie, have an adventure in the
   _____ located in _____.

2. For this adventure, Claudia is in charge of _____ and Jamie is in charge
   of_____.

3. In order to make money, Jamie has, for the past two years, _____
   when playing cards with his friend Brucie.

4. Claudia and Jamie join _____ for lectures and lunch at the
   Museum. They want to be _____.

5. At the closing and opening Museum times, the children hide in _____
   _____. They remain unseen by _____.

6. Claudia and Jamie join a line of people waiting to see the statue of an _____.
   This statue changes the focus of their _____.

7. Claudia soon decides that being _____ is the most
   inconvenient part of running away.

8. At the library, Claudia exhibits executive ability by assigning Jamie the task of
   _____. She will do the _____.

9. The nightly routine is interrupted on one occasion because the statue of Angel
   is _____.

10. While bathing in the water of the fountain located in the Museum restaurant, the
    children feel _____ with their feet. These are really _____.
    Jamie is delighted at the new source of _____.

Name_____

(Main Idea and Details)
Directions: Read the information and fill in each blank space with a word, words or phrase that will make the information given complete and true to the story.

Sample: The name of this novel is <u>*From the Mixed-Up Files of Mrs. Basil E. Frankweiler*</u>.

1.   The former owner of the statue of Angel was _____.

2.   The first clue that Claudia and Jamie discover about Angel is caused
     by_____.

3.   The children go to the Museum book store and find out that the M is Michelangelo's
     _____. This mark identifies him as the
     _____ of the marble.

4.   Claudia and Jamie decide to disclose their information to the _____
     _____ by writing a _____.

5.   To carry out their plan of disclosure, the children decide to rent _____
     _____ in order to _____
     _____.

6.   Because of the reply that they receive from Mr. Lowery of the Museum staff, Claudia
     and Jamie are _____ beyond words. Claudia feels that they
     have accomplished _____.

7.   Claudia's strong desire to go back to Greenwich feeling _____
     leads the children to make the quick decision to take the train to _____
     to interview _____.

8.   Claudia tells Mrs. Frankweiler that, to her, the fun part of running away from home was
     in the _____, not being discovered. However, after that
     became easy, it was _____ that became even more important
     than running away.

9.   The children find the secret of _____ in the files. It is a
     _____.

10. Claudia and Jamie decide to _____ Mrs. Frankweiler as their
     _____. She likes secrets, too!

Answer Key

Worksheet #9

1 True
2. False The City owns the building.
3. True
4. False The City provides for the Museum's heat, light, and power; and for about half the maintenance and security costs.
5. True

Worksheet #18

1. If the small square piece of the tangram square weighs one pound, what is the weight of the other six pieces? What is the total weight of the square? **small square=one pound; small triangle=1/2 pound each; medium triangle=one pound; parallelogram=one pound; large triangle=2 pounds each; total=8 pounds**

2. How much is the tangram square worth if the smallest triangle has a value of $1,000.00?—**$16,000.00 small triangle=$1,000; small square= $2,000; parallelogram= $2,000; large triangle= $4,000; medium triangle = $2,000**

3. What is the value of each piece of the tangram square if the whole square is worth $16.00? **smallest triangle =$1.00 each; square = $2.00; parallelogram = $2.00; medium triangle = $2.00; large triangle = $4.00 each**

4. If the smallest triangle of the tangram square has a value of 2/5 , what is the value of each piece of the tangram square? What is the total value of the square? **small triangle = 2/5; small square = 4/5; parallelogram = 4/5; medium triangle = 4/5; large triangle = 8/5 Total Value = (2) (2/5) + (3) (4/5) + (2) (8/5) = 4/5 + 12/5 + 16/5 = 32/5 or 6-2/5**

Quiz #1

1. Claudia Kincaid and younger brother, Jamie, have an adventure in the Metropolitan Museum of Art located in New York City.
2. For this adventure, Claudia is in charge of planning and Jamie is in charge of money.
3. In order to make money, Jamie has, for the past two years, cheated when playing cards with his friend Brucie.
4. Claudia and Jamie join school groups for lectures and lunch at the Museum. They want to be inconspicuous.
5. At the closing and opening Museum times, the children hide in washrooms. They remain unseen by standing on toilets.
6. Claudia and Jamie join a line of people waiting to see the statue of an Angel. This statue changes the focus of their adventure and study plan.
7. Claudia soon decides that being hungry is the most inconvenient part of running away.
8. At the library, Claudia exhibits executive ability by assigning Jamie the task of finding pictures of the statue, Angel. She will do the reading.
9. The nightly routine is interrupted on one occasion because the statue of Angel is relocated/moved.
10. While bathing in the water of the fountain located in the Museum restaurant, the children feel bumps with their feet. These are really coins. Jamie is delighted at the new source of revenue/money/income.

Quiz #2

1. The former owner of the statue of Angel was Mrs. Basil E. Frankweiler.
2. The first clue that Claudia and Jamie discover about Angel is caused by an *M* that had been chipped away in the marble on the bottom of the statue.
3. The children go to the Museum book store and find out that the M is Michelangelo's stonemason's mark. This mark identifies him as the owner of the marble.
4. Claudia and Jamie decide to disclose their information to the Head of the Museum by writing a letter.
5. To carry out their plan of disclosure, the children decide to rent a post office box in order to have a receptacle for the reply.
6. Because of the reply that they receive from Mr. Lowery of the Museum staff, Claudia and Jamie are disappointed beyond words. Claudia feels that they have accomplished nothing.
7. Claudia's strong desire to go back to Greenwich feeling different leads the children to make the quick decision to take the train to Farmington to interview Mrs. Basil E. Frankweiler.
8. Claudia tells Mrs. Frankweiler that, to her, the fun part of running away from home was in the hiding, not being discovered. However, after that became easy, it was Angel, the statue, that became even more important than running away.
9. The children find the secret of Angel in the files. It is a piece of paper. [On one side is a poem; on the other is a sketch of Angel, the statue. It is thought that the paper once belonged to Michelangelo.]
10. Claudia and Jamie decide to adopt Mrs. Frankweiler as their grandmother. She likes secrets, too!

Worksheet #12

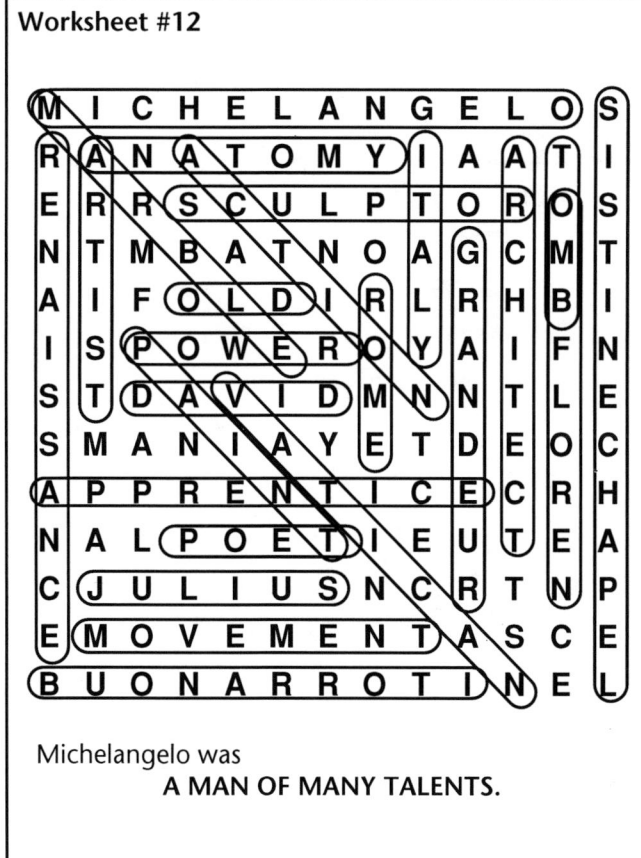

Michelangelo was
A MAN OF MANY TALENTS.

Worksheet #13

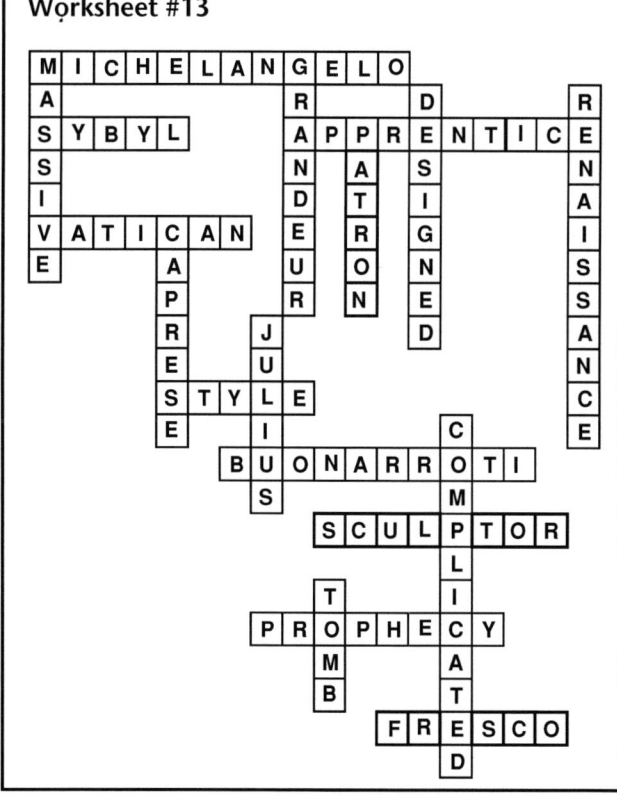

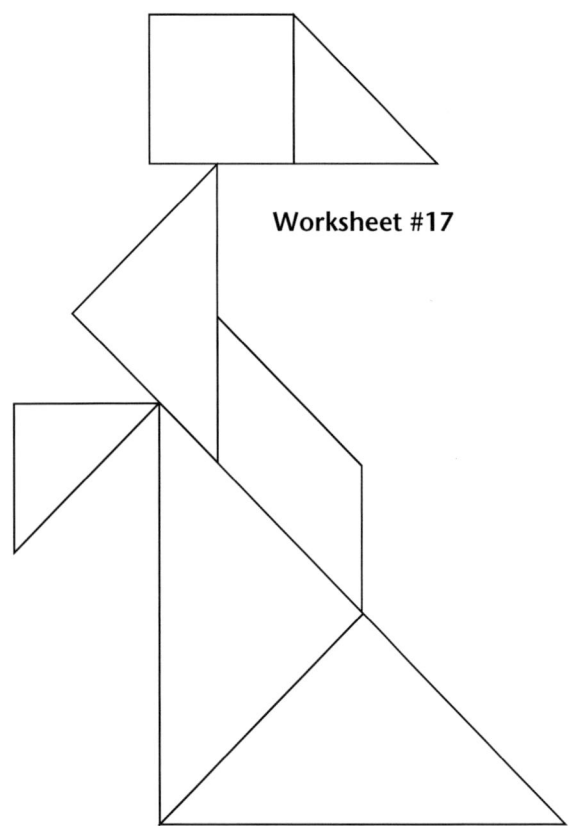

Worksheet #17

Worksheet #21

10   9   3   1   11   6   1   4

Worksheet #25

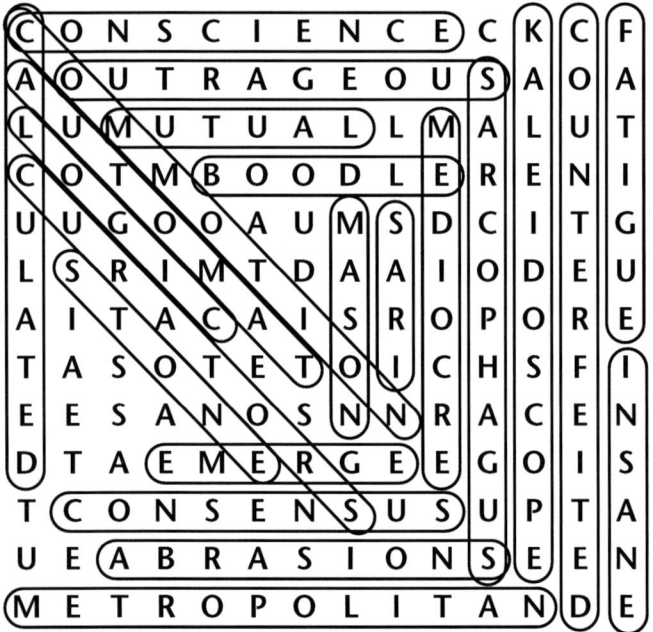

Hidden Message:
CLAUDIA SEES A STATUE.

Worksheet #26